Dear Parents/Caregivers:

Children learn to read in stages, and all children develop reading skills at different ages. **Fisher-Price® Ready Reader Storybooks**™ were created to encourage children's interest in reading and to increase their reading skills. The stories in this series were written to specific grade levels to serve the needs of children from preschool through third grade. Of course, every child is different, so we hope that you will allow your child to explore the stories at his or her own pace.

Book 1 and Book 2: Most Appropriate For Preschoolers

Book 3 and Book 4: Most Appropriate For Kindergartners

Book 5 and Book 6: Most Appropriate For First Graders

Book 7 and Book 8: Most Appropriate For Second Graders

Book 9 and Book 10: Most Appropriate For Third Graders

All of the stories in this series are fun, easy-to-follow tales that have engaging full-color artwork. Children can move from Books 1 and 2, which have the simplest vocabulary and concepts, to each progressive level to expand their reading skills. With the **Fisher-Price® Ready Reader Storybooks**™, reading will become an exciting adventure for your child. Soon your child will not only be ready to read, but will be eager to do so.

Educational Consultants: Mary McLean-Hely, M.A. in Education: Design and Evaluation of Educational Programs, Stanford University; Wendy Gelsanliter, M.S. in Early Childhood Education, Bank Street College of Education; Nancy A. Dearborn, B.S. in Education, University of Wisconsin-Whitewater

Fisher-Price® Ready Reader Storybook ™

Ed Can Help (Book 3)

Written by Sallianne Spatafore • Illustrated by Diana Zourelias

Modern Publishing
A Division of Unisystems, Inc.
New York, New York 10022

Now that Ed is six, he can help at home.

Ed likes to help.

Ed helps his dad look for the car key.

After they find it, they go
out for ice cream!

Ed's mom likes to
work in the garden.

Ed helps her pull the weeds.

13

Ed helps his sister Nell write letters.

Nell is learning fast.

Ed shows his
brother Ned how
to tie his shoes.

Ed and Nell carry
the newspapers
outside. "Here
comes the truck,"
Nell says.

Nell helps Ed clean his room.

Then Ed and Nell have
time to play.

Ed's sister Belle helps him
with his homework.
They work on math.

Everyone helps
set the table.

SMIL

24

Ed puts out the plates. Ned and Nell fold the napkins.

Ed and Belle help bake
a cake.

In Ed's house, all of the kids have jobs to do. And now that Ed is six, he can help a lot.